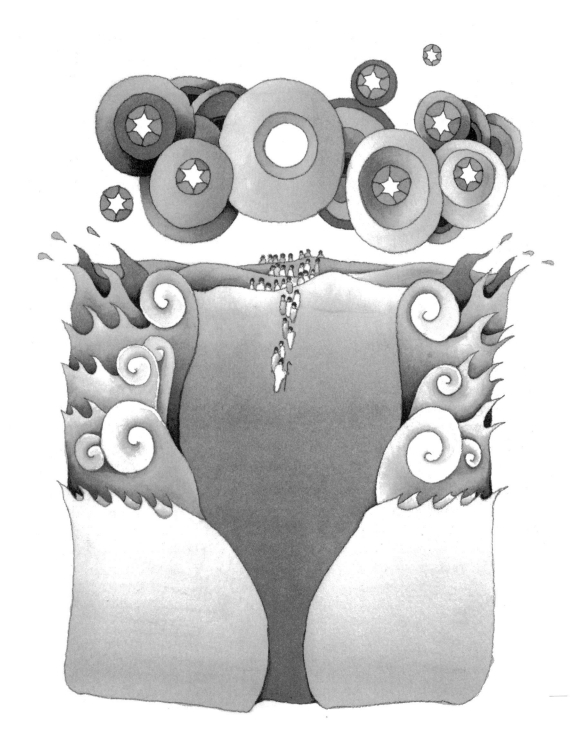

How You Can Use This Haggadah

The Family Haggadah is written to help families with children enjoy celebrating their Seder—the ritual meal on the first and second nights of Passover.

Haggadah means "telling," and *The Family Haggadah* is designed to help you and your children participate actively in this ancient Jewish tradition. This book will help you retell the Passover story during your Seder, using the traditional signs and symbols that have helped Jews remember the events and meaning of our Exodus from Egypt for more than three thousand years. I hope these experiences will help you to discover for yourself some of the deeper meanings and mysteries of this joyous festival.

Try to involve your children as much as possible—to the extent you feel comfortable. *Specific suggestions about ways to help children participate before and during your Seder can be found on pages 64–66.* Choose the activities that best fit your family. Feel free to change, omit, or incorporate moments that will make your Seder more understandable and meaningful to you and your family.

The central purpose of the Seder is to help us and our children experience the Exodus in a very personal way. Your own interpretations and variations of tradition will help create the memories your children carry with them into the future.

Before you begin your Seder, decide who will serve as your leader this year—someone to help direct discussions, encourage active participation by guests of all ages, and ensure order while keeping a watchful eye on the clock.

But please, don't automatically choose the oldest male for this key role. Be creative about choosing an appropriate leader each year: A child near Bar or Bat Mitzvah age? An older aunt or grandmother with a gift for making each guest feel essential and welcome? Someone celebrating a birthday or anniversary? Be sure to choose a leader who can help each guest participate comfortably in the experience you are all creating together.

The Family Haggadah deliberately avoids sexist, patriarchal, or militaristic language, usage, and customs. The Four Sons are now the Four Children. God is not described as either male or female but as a Being of limitless creativity and power. Such changes reflect the desire to keep Jewish tradition relevant and alive.

Questions are at the heart of every Seder. In fact, the Seder is designed to answer the beloved, melodious Four Questions—as well as to ask and grapple with others that may arise. Please encourage questions, interpretations, and opinions from everyone at your table. Remember that there is no right answer, especially to the most important questions, and that each participant can make valuable contributions regardless of age or familiarity with Jewish tradition.

Also bear in mind that the unofficial Fifth Question is often

"When do we eat?" so be sensitive about when enough is enough.

A few brief notes about *The Family Haggadah*:

• Read through "The Night Before Your Seder" (pages 4–7) and "How Children Can Participate in Your Seder" (pages 64–66), then make appropriate preparations for the activites you choose.

• Before the Seder begins, the leader should take some time to become familiar with the text and rituals.

• *The Family Haggadah* is meant to be read aloud by the leader and all other willing participants. The easiest way is to go around the table taking turns.

• It probably will be most effective if one skilled reader or adult reads aloud the Story of Moses, the Ten Plagues, and the Exodus.

• Everyone should feel welcome to join in the prayers, blessings, and songs, which are meant to be read or sung aloud together. Traditional texts appear in English, Hebrew, and Hebrew transliteration, so you can choose which works best for your family.

The Night Before
Your Seder

Hametz

Tomorrow night, as the sun sets, Passover begins: the holiday we celebrate each spring to remember how God saved the Jewish people from slavery in the land of Egypt. Tomorrow night we will tell the whole story and try to make it come alive so we can feel it is happening all over again to us.

But tonight we have another very important thing to do: we have to search for *hametz* (kha-METZ or KHO-metz). Any bread or food made of wheat, barley, or rye combined with leaven or yeast and allowed to rise is called *hametz* in Hebrew. This includes most kinds of cake, crackers, pie, pastry, pasta, cookies, and breakfast cereal. Some people also include rice, millet, corn, and legumes. The rules about *hametz* (and foods that are labeled "Kosher for Passover") are complicated. You can ask a rabbi questions about these rules if you like, or you may want to ask somebody in your family to help you understand how and why they observe the rules about *hametz*.

Before tomorrow night, we must remove all *hametz* from our home until the week of Passover is over. Why?

When the children of Israel had to leave Egypt, there was no time for bread to rise. To help us remember their escape or Exodus, we eat no *hametz* during the Passover holiday. And we keep no bread—not even a crumb—anywhere in the house.

Getting rid of *hametz* makes the matzah (ma-TZAH or MA-tzoh; plural, *matzot*—ma-TZOT) we eat during Passover special. Matzah is the flat bread made without leaven that the Israelites ate during the time they fled from slavery in Egypt. Eliminating *hametz* is a way of getting rid of the old and making room for the new.

In keeping with tradition, we give our *hametz* away to hungry people, then clean very, very carefully to get rid of any crumbs. But just in case we missed some, we'll search for *hametz* tonight after sundown with a flashlight or candle, a wooden spoon, a long feather, and a bag to collect the crumbs we find.

The grown-ups (children can help) can break a slice of bread into ten pieces, then hide these scraps of hametz for the children to find. This provides ample opportunities for a successful search.

SEARCHING FOR CRUMBS

First, let's turn out the lights. We'll use this flashlight or candle to help us find all the *hametz*. We'll search for every last crumb of *hametz*—even the tiniest ones scattered into the darkest corners of the closets, cupboards, or strollers. Before we search, we say this prayer:

Blessed are You, Eternal God, Creator of the universe,
who makes us holy through Your commandments and
commands us to remove all hametz.

Shhh! Don't say a word! Let's search quietly, without even whispering. It's important to find every crumb and all ten hidden pieces of *hametz* before Passover begins. We'll use the feather to sweep the crumbs into the wooden spoon, then save all the *hametz* in the bag until we can burn it tomorrow morning.

After the Search

Do you think we found every last crumb of hametz? Probably not. After all, we're not perfect; we're human. Here's a prayer we can say together about any crumbs we missed:

If there are any crumbs I haven't seen or taken away, I
hereby disown them. I declare them to be nothing—as
ownerless as the dust of the earth.

No one can be perfect. We can never get rid of every crumb or stop making mistakes. All we can do is try. Searching for *hametz* is a way of trying.

The Day of the Seder

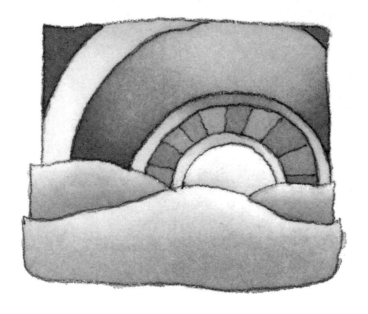

Preparing the Seder Plate

We need the following foods for our Seder plate, which will have a place of honor on our table. Each of the foods has a special meaning that helps tell the Passover story.

Zeroa (ze-ro-AH)—a roasted shank or chicken bone. Vegetarians and those who prefer may use a roasted beet.

> Place the bone or beet under your broiler till it looks brown and scorched.

Maror (ma-ROAR)—bitter herbs.

> You can use a dish of red or white store-bought horseradish

or a fresh horseradish root cut into slivers (very interesting, dramatic, and bitter enough to make your eyes water!).

Haroset (kha-RO-set)—a mixture of apples, nuts, sweet wine, and cinnamon.

> You can make *haroset* by dicing six to eight apples, then adding a half cup of chopped walnuts or almonds, and a generous amount of cinnamon. (Because this dish is so popular and tastes even better as a leftover, figure on at least half an apple per guest). Add enough red Passover wine or grape juice to form the mixture into a thick, chunky paste. Every family seems to have its own favorite version of *haroset*, so experiment until you find yours. Some alternatives: add honey or diced dried apricots or dates.

Hazeret (kha-ZER-et)—additional *maror*, usually romaine lettuce.

Karpas (kar-PAS)—fresh greens such as parsley or watercress.

Baytzah (bay-TSAH)—a roasted egg.

> Place a hard-boiled egg (peeled or in the shell), under a broiler till it looks brown and scorched.

Prepare salt water for dipping herbs by dissolving one or two teaspoons of salt per cup of warm water. Some families make several larger bowls to pass around; others prefer making individual cups or small bowls for each guest (children enjoy having their own private bowl).

Setting Your Seder Table

You can use this checklist as a guide for preparing your holiday table. You will need:

◇ A pitcher of water, a large bowl, and hand towels for ritual hand washing. (Place on or near your dining table.)

◇ One or more pairs of candleholders and candles. (Long, slender tapers will last longer than regular Sabbath candles.)

◇ One or more bowls or individual cups of salt water for dipping herbs.

◇ Three *matzot* under a matzah cover.

◇ An *Afikoman* holder: an envelope, napkin, or some kind of holder to prevent scattering crumbs during the ritual of hiding and finding the special piece of matzah that concludes the meal.

◇ Elijah's cup, either filled with wine or empty so that all participants can contribute some of their own wine to welcome Elijah the Prophet (see page 54).

◇ Miriam's cup, either filled with water or left empty to be filled with water from each person's water goblet (see page 42).

◇ Decanters or bottles of Passover wine and/or grape juice (to be used by children and other guests as a nonalcoholic alternative whenever the text mentions wine).

◇ Generous bowls of additional *karpas*, *maror*, and *haroset* to pass and share (see page 9).

◇ Pillows (if possible, for each person) to lean on during the Seder.

◇ Flowers are optional but help make your table especially beautiful and festive. If necessary, trim so the blossoms don't obscure people's line of vision.

◇ The Seder Plate (see page 9).

◇ A place setting for each person, with a wine cup and water glass. If you like, use place cards to indicate seating arrangements.

This can be a night to use your finest heirloom china, crystal, and silver. Sharing the family stories and fond memories that make these objects precious and give them personal meaning will help your children begin to understand their symbolic value.

On the other hand, this is not the night to worry about jeopardizing Great-Grandma's heirlooms with an accident-waiting-to-happen. Especially if you expect very young children, you may decide to use paper and plastic so you can concentrate on what really matters: the celebration itself.

And just a reminder: everyone should wait to eat any matzah until after saying the blessing and starting the actual Passover meal.

A Few More Suggestions

Here are some additional tips to help make your Seder a pleasant event, especially if you have very young children:

◇ Encourage young children to nap in the afternoon so they can stay up late to enjoy the festivities.

◇ Prepare inexpensive gifts as rewards for finding the *Afikoman* (see page 53).

◇ Serve a substantial late afternoon snack to help tide everyone over until dinner is served (probably much later than usual).

◇ Invite your guests to arrive thirty to forty-five minute before you plan to begin your Seder (traditionally after sunset). This provides ample time for welcomes, introductions, and storing coats and strollers.

◇ Prepare platters of crudités (cut-up fresh vegetables—carrots, celery, Jerusalem artichoke, broccoli, cauliflower, etc.) served with kosher-for-Passover dips and chips, to eat with the *Karpas*.

Generous portions will quell your guests' hunger pangs and make it easier for people to enjoy the Seder before the actual meal is served.

◇ When you're ready to begin, the hosts and leader can invite everyone to gather at the table to begin your Seder by lighting the candles together.

The Seder Begins

Beginning the Seder

The sun is now hidden, and the full moon is rising. It is time to begin our Seder: our telling of the Passover story in a special way, and in a special order.

The story we tell tonight isn't a fairy tale that happened "once upon a time." It's a true story. And as we create our Seder celebration together, we will help it happen tonight to each of us.

The Seder tells the story of how we were slaves in Egypt before God led us to freedom with signs and wonders. Passover—the Exodus from Egypt—didn't happen once and only once, to someone else in some other place. Each year at Passover we go on a journey in our hearts from slavery to freedom, from sadness to joy—just as every year we journey from the cold and darkness of winter to the warmth and light of spring.

Tonight, in our home and other homes, in this neighborhood and others, all across the country, in countries all over our planet, families of Jews and their friends are beginning their Seder and lighting their candles. Imagine them joining us at one huge table that stretches across the world; imagine the flames of all our candles, countless as the stars in the sky.

The Hebrew word *Seder* (say-der; plural, se-dah-reem) means "order." *Haggadah* (ha-ga-dah; plural, ha-ga-dote) means "telling." When we read this Haggadah at our Passover Seder, we are retelling the story of the Exodus in a specific order.

It is a story that begins in slavery and ends in freedom, starts with sadness and ends with joy, begins in darkness and ends in light.

Lighting the Candles

Let us recite together the blessing for lighting the candles. Then watch how the glow of our candles changes everything we see.

Blessing for Lighting the Candles

Blessed are You, Eternal God, Creator of the universe, who makes our lives holy with Your commandments, and commands us to kindle these holiday lights.

בָּרוּךְ אַתָּה יְיָ אֱלֹהֵינוּ מֶלֶךְ
הָעוֹלָם, אֲשֶׁר קִדְּשָׁנוּ בְּמִצְוֹתָיו וְצִוָּנוּ
לְהַדְלִיק נֵר שֶׁל יוֹם טוֹב.

Ba-RUKH A-TAH A-do-NAI, E-lo-HAY-nu, ME-lekh
ha-O-LAM a-SHER kid-SHA-nu b'MITZ-VO-TAV
v'tsee-VA-nu l'had-LEEK ner shel Yom Tov.

May each of us help kindle flames of hope and freedom, and
bring light to the world.

Let's thank God for the continuing miracle of being alive, and
for the blessing of being together tonight.

Blessed are You, Eternal God, Creator of the universe,
who has given us life, kept us in life, and enabled us to
reach this season of joy.

בָּרוּךְ אַתָּה יְיָ אֱלֹהֵינוּ מֶלֶךְ
הָעוֹלָם שֶׁהֶחֱיָנוּ וְקִיְּמָנוּ וְהִגִּיעָנוּ
לַזְּמַן הַזֶּה.

Ba-RUKH A-TAH A-do-NAI, E-lo-HAY-nu, ME-lekh
ha-O-LAM, she-HE-khe-YA-nu, v'KEE-ma-nu v'HEE-gee-ah-nu
la-z'MAN ha-ZEH.

The First Cup of Wine

We say a prayer of thanks before we drink the first cup of wine (or grape juice).

Blessing for the Wine (Kiddush)

Blessed are You, Eternal God, Creator of the universe, who creates the fruit of the vine.

בָּרוּךְ אַתָּה יְיָ אֱלֹהֵינוּ מֶלֶךְ
הָעוֹלָם בּוֹרֵא פְּרִי הַגָּפֶן.

Ba-RUKH A-TAH A-do-NAI, E-lo-HAY-nu, ME-lekh ha-o-LAM, bo-RAY pree ha-GAH-fen.

Washing Our Hands

LEADER:

According to ancient custom, we wash our hands, but no blessing is recited. Washing our hands is a way of showing that we hope to purify our hearts, and not just our hands. It is also a way of feeling clean and ready to take part in our Seder.

Either pass a pitcher, bowl, and hand towels around the table or appoint someone to carry them from person to person.

DIPPING THE GREENS OR *Karpas*

These fresh new greens or *karpas* (kar-PAS) are signs of spring. They remind us of all the little green stems quietly and secretly pushing up out of the earth now that the long, cold winter is over. The *karpas* remind us that each year in spring, the earth is reborn.

Dipping *karpas* in salt water reminds us of all the tears cried by our people when we were slaves in Egypt. The salt water also reminds us of the many children, women, and men who are still slaves right now, today. They cry enough tears in one day to fill this bowl to overflowing. We dip our greens in salt and water as a way of paying attention to their tears.

LEADER:

Everyone may now take some greens and get ready to dip them in salt water. We recite together:

Blessing for the Greens

Blessed are You, Eternal God, Creator of the universe,
who gives us the fruit of the earth.

בָּרוּךְ אַתָּה יְיָ אֱלֹהֵינוּ מֶלֶךְ
הָעוֹלָם בּוֹרֵא פְּרִי הָאֲדָמָה.

Ba-RUKH A-TAH A-do-NAI, E-lo-HAY-nu, ME-lekh
ha-o-LAM, bo-RAY pree ha-ah-da-MAH.

It was a common custom in ancient times to begin meals with fresh vegetable hors d'oeuvres—which is the source of the ritual of dipping *karpas*. Please help revive this ancient tradition by helping yourselves to these vegetables, chips, and dips as we continue our Seder.

Don't forget to lean back while you eat! In ancient times, slaves could not relax and feast peacefully together. As you lean comfortably, remember that you are no longer a slave but a free person.

HIDING THE *Afikoman*

LEADER:

Now it is time for a special game of hide-and-seek. We must hide the *Afikoman* (ah-fee-ko-man)—a piece of matzah that will be the very last thing we eat at the end of our Seder meal.

I will take these three *matzot* and break the middle matzah in half. We will put one piece between the two remaining *matzot*.

The other, larger piece will be the Afikoman. Cover your eyes while the grown-ups hide it for the children to find . . . [*or* The children can hide it so the grown-ups can search.] Much later tonight we will need to find the Afikoman so that we can complete our Seder meal.

In either case, the leader or host should establish simple rules about where the *Afikoman* can or cannot be hidden, making certain rooms (like the kitchen or bathroom) and certain places (like closets or cabinets) off-limits.

This matzah is the bread of affliction—the bread of poverty and sorrow—that our ancestors ate when they were slaves in the land of Egypt.

What is matzah? Special bread made without leaven or yeast so it cannot rise. Why do we eat matzah on Passover? Because matzah reminds us that we had to escape from Egypt so quickly that there was no time for bread to rise. It also reminds us of the

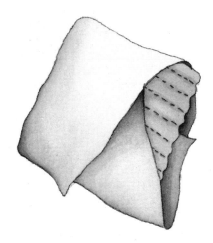

poor food we ate when we were slaves. Breaking the matzah into pieces reminds us that when we were hungry, we had very little to eat. When we were slaves, we never had enough food to save for later.

LEADER:

Someone please open our door as we say these words together:

> *Let anyone who is hungry come and eat. Let anyone who is a stranger, anyone homeless or poor, share with us the hope of Passover. For we know how it feels to be a stranger in a strange land.*

Let's each decide how we can share what we have with other people. What could you do? If you like, you can tell your ideas to the rest of us.

The Meaning of the Seder Plate

Tonight we will all eat foods from the Seder plate—the most important plate at our table. Tasting and talking about these Passover foods will help us make our journey out of Egypt tonight. I will show you each ingredient as it is named and explained:

Zeroa (ze-ro-AH) is the roasted shank bone [*or* roasted beet]. It reminds us of the sacrifice of the Passover lamb, and of God's instructions to mark our doorposts with its blood. It also reminds us that when all the firstborn sons of the Egyptians were slain, God *passed over* the homes of the Children of Israel.

Maror (ma-ROAR) means bitter herbs, like horseradish. *Maror* reminds us of the bitterness and pain of slavery.

Haroset (kha-RO-set) is a mixture of chopped apples, nuts, wine, and spices. It reminds us of the bricks and mortar Jewish slaves had to make when they built cities for Pharaoh in Egypt.

Hazeret (kha-ZER-et) is also *maror*, usually romaine lettuce. These additional bitter herbs can be used to make a "Hillel sandwich"—*maror* and *haroset* between two pieces of matzah—at the appropriate point in the Seder.

Karpas (kar-PAS) is a green vegetable like parsley or watercress. It reminds us of spring and rebirth.

Baytzah (bay-TZAH) is the roasted, hard-boiled egg. It is a symbol of birth and life. It also reminds us of the offerings our ancestors made long ago when they prayed in the Temple in Jerusalem to give thanks for their fertile fields and flocks.

WHY IS THIS NIGHT DIFFERENT FROM ALL OTHER NIGHTS?

LEADER:

This is a night to question; this is a night to wonder. We will now ask the Four Questions—questions we will answer as we retell the Seder story.

According to tradition, the youngest child asks these four ancient questions. Tonight, they can be asked the youngest or by all the children together . . . or by anyone who volunteers.

The Four Questions

Why is this night different from all other nights?

On all other nights, we eat leavened bread or matzah; tonight we eat only matzah. Why?

מַה נִּשְׁתַּנָּה הַלַּיְלָה הַזֶּה מִכָּל הַלֵּילוֹת:

שֶׁבְּכָל הַלֵּילוֹת אָנוּ אוֹכְלִין חָמֵץ וּמַצָּה,
הַלַּיְלָה הַזֶּה כֻּלּוֹ מַצָּה.

Mah nish-ta-NAH ha-LAI-lah ha-ZEH mi-KOL ha-lay-LOT?

Sheh-b'KHOL ha-lay-LOT A-nu okh-LEEN ha-METZ
u'ma-TZAH. Ha-LAI-lah ha-ZEH ku-LO ma-TZAH.

On all other nights, we eat any kind of vegetable; tonight we must eat bitter herbs. Why?

שֶׁבְּכָל הַלֵּילוֹת אָנוּ אוֹכְלִין שְׁאָר יְרָקוֹת,
הַלַּיְלָה הַזֶּה מָרוֹר.

Sheh-b'KHOL ha-lay-LOT A-nu okh-LEEN sh'AR y'ra-KOT.
Ha-LAI-lah ha-ZEH ma-ROR.

*On all other nights, we do not dip herbs even once; tonight
we dip twice. Why?*

שֶׁבְּכָל הַלֵּילוֹת אֵין אָנוּ מַטְבִּילִין
אֲפִילוּ פַּעַם אֶחָת,
הַלַּיְלָה הַזֶּה שְׁתֵּי פְעָמִים.

Sheh-b'KHOL ha-lay-LOT ayn A-nu mat-bee-LEEN a-FEE-lu
PA-ahm eh-KHAT. Ha-LAI-lah ha-ZEH sh'tay f'a-MEEM.

*On all other nights we sit up straight or recline on pillows;
tonight we must lean on pillows. Why?*

שֶׁבְּכָל הַלֵּילוֹת אָנוּ אוֹכְלִין
בֵּין יוֹשְׁבִין וּבֵין מְסֻבִּין,
הַלַּיְלָה הַזֶּה כֻּלָּנוּ מְסֻבִּין.

Sheh-b'KHOL ha-lay-LOT A-nu okh-LEEN bayn yosh-VEEN
u-VAYN m'su-BEEN. Ha-LAI-lah ha-ZEH ku-LA-nu m'su-BEEN.

So many questions! Listen, as our Seder begins to help us find
answers. But don't expect to hear all the answers: there are some
questions only you can answer. And there are some questions
with no answers at all.

Mah Nishtanah

Traditional Israeli
arr. Rogerio Marx

Mah nish-ta-nah ha-lai-lah ha-zeh mi-

kol ha-lay-lot, mi-kol ha-lay-

lot?
1. She-b'-khol ha-lay-lot a-nu okh-leen ha-
2. She-b'-khol ha-lay-lot a-nu okh-leen sh'-
3. She-b'-khol ha-lay-lot ayn a-nu mat-bee-leen a-
4. She-b'-khol ha-lay-lot a-nu okh-leen bayn yosh-

metz u'-ma-tzah, ha-metz u'-ma-
ar y'-ra-kot, sh'-ar y'-ra-
fee-lu pa' am e-khat, a-fee-lu pa' am e-
veen u-vayn m'-su been, bayn yosh-veen-u-vayn m'su

tzah. Ha-lai-lah ha-zeh ha-lai-lah ha-zeh ku-
kot. Ha-lai-lah ha-zeh ha-lai-lah ha-zeh ma-
khat. Ha-lai-lah ha-zeh ha-lai-lah ha-zeh sh'-
been. Ha-lai-lah ha-zeh ha-lai-lah ha-zeh ku-

1.
lo ma-tzah. Ha
ror ma-ror. Ha
tay-f'-a-meem. Ha
la-nu m'-su-been. Ha

2.
tzah.
ror.
meem.
been.

• 27 •

The Four Children: Which One Are You?

Every child is different. Each person is different and hears the Passover story differently. Which kind of child are you? Do you have a little of each child in you? Or are you some other kind of child?

The **Wise Child** is curious and asks, "What did God tell *us* to do on Passover? And what does it all mean to *us*?" We try to teach this child everything we know.

The **Wicked or Selfish Child** doesn't know or care about Passover. This child says, "What does all this mean to *you*? And what does it matter, anyway?" We tell this child that we celebrate Passover because we feel God freed *each* of us from slavery. We try to help this child find a personal meaning in the Passover story.

The **Simple or Innocent Child** says, "What's going on? Why are you doing all this?" We give this child a simple answer: we have Passover "because God worked wonders for *me* when I went forth from Egypt." Each person says *me* because tonight each one of us is a slave waiting to be free.

And for the **Child Who Doesn't Know How to Ask Questions?** We tell the story of Passover even to the smallest child or to people unable to ask questions, so that we can all remember what a blessing it is that God took us out of Egypt.

The Passover Story

Our story begins in sorrow and ends in glory. It is the story of how God saved us with signs and wonders, just as God promises to save us from enemies that rise up against us in every age. As we tell the story of Passover, imagine it is happening all over again—to you—tonight.

It is long, long ago, and we are slaves in Egypt. We work very hard all day, every day, in the scorching sun, making millions of bricks and tons of mortar to build treasure cities for Pharaoh, the king of Egypt.

It is very hard, very bitter to be a slave. We can't rest when we're tired or drink when we're thirsty; we get no pay; the overseers beat us. Every day we sweat in the blazing sun, our muscles straining and screaming. No matter how long and hard we work, we never finish.

Still, we believe God will rescue us. We refuse to stop living just because Pharaoh wants us dead.

Then Pharaoh begins to become afraid of us. He decides there are too many of us, and gives a cruel command: "All Israelite boys must be drowned in the river as soon as they are born." But some women won't follow Pharaoh's orders; they listen to God and not to the king of Egypt. One of these women is Yocheved.

The Story of Moses

Amram and Yocheved have a baby despite Pharaoh's cruel decree. As soon as Yocheved sees her tiny son, she decides to hide him. When he's three months old and too big to keep quiet, she weaves a big basket and smears it with tar to make it waterproof. Tenderly, she kisses her baby, tucks him carefully into the little boat she made, and puts it into the river Nile.

The baby's sister, Miriam, follows the basket as it floats down the river—right to the spot where the daughter of Pharaoh is swimming.

Pharaoh's daughter hears the baby cry. She defies her father's cruel law and rescues the child from drowning, even though she suspects he's an Israelite. She names him Moses, which means "drawn from the water," and raises him in the royal palace as her own son.

Miriam is very clever: she brings her mother to Pharaoh's daughter. Yocheved offers to help feed and care for the baby. This way, she can raise her own son. She will teach him in secret about his people.

Moses grows up in Pharaoh's palace, living like a prince in ease and luxury. But it makes him angry and sad to see how the Israelites suffer.

One day, after Moses grows to be a man, he sees an Egyptian beating an Israelite slave. Moses is so filled with rage that he kills the Egyptian and hides the body in the sand. When Pharaoh finds out, he threatens to punish the murderer with death. Moses is frightened and runs away.

Then, in the midst of the wilderness, God speaks to Moses in flames of fire. The flames flash up out of a burning bush that burns and burns, but is not consumed.

God tells Moses, "Behold, I hear the cry of the children of

Israel. I have surely remembered you and seen what is done to you. And now I will put forth My hand and smite Egypt with signs and with wonders. Go, tell Pharaoh:

Let My people go!"

LEADER:
Each time these words appear, everyone can say them together:

Let My people go!

And each time God sends a plague, imagine it is happening to the Egyptians tonight—right in front of your very eyes.

The Ten Plagues

Now Moses tells Pharaoh,

Let My people go!

But Pharaoh says no. So God sends ten terrible plagues to punish the Egyptians; to show Pharaoh that only God is God.

First, God turns all the water in all the rivers, streams, ponds, and pools in Egypt to blood. For seven days, blood flows everywhere; there isn't a single drop of water for the Egyptians to drink. And God says again,

Let My people go!

Pharaoh still refuses. Now God sends frogs swarming all over Egypt. Frogs hop into the Egyptians' houses, into their bedrooms, into their beds. They hop into the kitchens where the bread is made, and even into the ovens.

Let My people go!

Pharaoh promises to set us free. But as soon as God makes all the frogs hop away, Pharaoh breaks his promise.

So God makes a new plague, and turns all the dust of the earth into gnats and flies. They buzz and bite the Egyptian beasts, and crawl all over Pharaoh and his people. The Egyptians can hardly breathe. And God says:

Let My people go!

Pharaoh promises to set us free. But his heart is hard and he breaks his promise again. God sends a disease to kill all the Egyptian horses, donkeys, and camels. It kills every flock and herd of the Egyptians, but not one of our cattle dies.

Let My people go!

But Pharaoh is stubborn; he still won't let us go.
And now God tells Moses and his brother Aaron to take handfuls of soot from the furnace and throw them up into the sky. Wherever the soot falls, painful boils break out all over the bodies of the Egyptians and their animals.

Let My people go!

But Pharaoh's heart is hard, and he still refuses to let the Children of Israel go.

Then God sends a storm of thunder, lightning, and hail: the worst storm ever known in the land of Egypt. Hail hits like hammers; fire and thunder run down to earth, shattering trees, falling everywhere, striking everything—except us.

Let My people go!

But as soon as the wild storm is over, Pharaoh again hardens his heart.

So God sends a plague of locusts. They cover the earth and darken the land. They eat every leaf on every tree, and every blade of grass. They fill the houses; they eat every piece of fruit and grain till there is nothing green or growing anywhere in all of Egypt.

Let My people go!

When Pharaoh begs forgiveness and swears to free us, God sends a strong wind. It picks up all the locusts and blows them into the sea. But again Pharaoh's heart is hard.

Let My people go!

And now God sends darkness down upon Egypt, darkness so thick you can touch it with your hands. For three whole days, the Egyptians are wrapped in darkness thicker than blankets; they cannot even see one another. Yet our homes are full of light.

Let My people go!

When Pharaoh still refuses, God sends the tenth and final plague.

But first, God tells us to use the blood of a lamb to mark our doors. Then the Angel of Death will see the mark on our doors and pass over our houses when it is time to inflict the plague.

God also instructs us to roast and eat the lamb that night with matzah and maror, unleavened bread and bitter herbs, and to eat this food fully dressed, with sandals on our feet, ready to travel.

Now it is midnight. God enters the land of Egypt to slay the firstborn of every Egyptian family: from the firstborn son of Pharaoh, to the firstborn among his servants, to the firstborn among the prisoners in the dungeons, to the firstborn cattle. All fall dead.

But God sees the blood on our doors, and the Angel of Death *passes over* our houses.

Let My people go!

Then finally, finally, Pharaoh frees us and tells us, "Rise up and go, and bless me also."

The Exodus

LEADER:

And now it is time to leave: time for our Exodus. Take a bite of matzah; then close your eyes and see.

Look: the moon is a round white circle. It pours bright silver through the open window. Listen: the fire snaps in the quiet. Everyone is sleeping. There is a sudden rush of wind or wings.

And now screams pierce the quiet. They are the cries of the

Egyptian fathers and mothers as they discover their firstborn sons—dead.

We hear a knock at the door. Voices call softly through the dark: "Hurry! Pharaoh says he will let us go. But we must leave now. No time to pack clothes or toys, no time to prepare food. No time to bake bread, or even let the dough rise. We must escape quickly, before Pharaoh changes his mind again."

We run through the shadows, clutching each others' hands to stay together. We can still see the full moon glowing in the hot black sky. The sad cries of the Egyptians still ring in the distance. We stumble along as quickly as we can, rushing through the night with all the other Israelite families. There are thousands and thousands of us.

We walk all night, and it seems the night will never end. Our legs ache. The stones rub blisters on our toes. Our stomachs growl for food. Our mouths are dry and full of dust.

The sun rises, burning hot. We're too tired to take one more step. We have to stop for a short rest. The children are crying for food; even the grown-ups are exhausted and hungry.

Soon the air is hot as an oven. We all help mix flour and water for bread. There's no time to let it rise, so we put it on the scorching rocks to bake quickly in the sun.

It's time to walk again before there's time to eat, but we're so hungry we eat on the run. The sunbaked matzah is the best bread we've ever tasted. Even though it's dry and flat; even though it crumbles in our mouths; even though it's mixed with desert sand

and the dust of the road, it is the bread of freedom.

By day and by night we walk through the wilderness. But we are never alone and we never lose our way. For God leads us by day with a pillar of cloud, and by night with a pillar of fire.

And just when we know we cannot take another step, we smell water. We hear waves on the shore. The Sea of Reeds, the Red Sea, glitters before us, stretching farther than our eyes can see.

But what's that pounding above the sound of the sea? Horses? Soldiers? Yes: Pharaoh has changed his mind one last time. And now more than six hundred chariots appear on the horizon— soldiers coming to take us back into slavery. We are caught between the soldiers and the sea.

"O God, help us!" we cry. And God hears us and saves us, with signs and with wonders. The Angel of God, who is leading us, moves behind us. The pillar of fire moves between the army of Israel and the army of the Egyptians to keep them apart.

Now, as we watch, God makes the east wind blow the waters of the sea apart. The sea splits before us.

Now there is a path right through the middle of the water: a wide, dry pathway we can follow to freedom. But is it safe? How can we be sure the sea won't crash down and drown us?

We hold each other tight. We can see the moonlight turning the wet sand to silver where the waters part. We can see the moonlight blazing on the glassy walls of the frozen sea, still as stone on both sides of the path. We can hear Pharaoh's chariots thunder closer. We know it is time.

Now! Quickly! We step on the path in the middle of the sea; we run as fast as we can into the moonlit miracle. And the hand of God holds back the water till we reach the other side.

But look: Pharaoh's horses, soldiers, and chariots are right behind us, charging toward us on the path through the sea. Is it too late? Will they catch us—and kill us?

God lets the waters go. The sea crashes down on the horses, soldiers, and chariots; it swallows them up. They sink like stones.

It is over. It is only beginning. We are safe. Moses sings a song of praise and the men join him. Miriam jingles her tambourine, leaping and singing, leading the women in a joyful dance of praise and celebration.

Dayenu!
It Would Have Been Enough For Us

LEADER:

Let's sing and dance and celebrate with them. Let's sing a song of victory, and praise our mighty God. Let's sing *"Dayenu."*

The word *Dayenu* means "it would have been enough for us." We would be grateful for even one of God's miracles, but there are so many.

Had God brought us out of Egypt but not divided the sea for us . . .
Had God divided the sea but not let us cross . . .
　It would have been enough for us! Dayenu!
Had God let us cross the sea but not kept us forty years in the desert . . .
Had God fed us manna but not given us the Sabbath . . .
　It would have been enough for us! Dayenu!
Had God given us the Sabbath but not brought us to Mount Sinai . . .
Had God led us into the Land of Israel but not built the Temple . . .
　It would have been enough for us! Dayenu!

LEADER:

Can you tell about some of the things, people, or events that make you feel grateful? Are they ordinary blessings, or miracles? Can you make them into a song that fits the tune of *"Dayenu"*?

Miriam's Cup: A New Tradition

We can pause here after our song and celebration to observe a new tradition with many old meanings. Think back to the story we are telling tonight and remember: There would have been no Exodus, no Passover, no Seder, no freedom without the many brave women who played crucial roles in the Passover drama. There would have been no Exodus without Shifrah and Puah, the

Dayenu!

Traditional
arr. Rogerio Marx

1. Ee- lu ho- tzee ho- tzee- a - nu, ho- tzee- a - nu me- mitz- ra - yim
2. Ee- lu ho- tzee ho- tzee a - nu, ho- tzee- a - nu me- mitz- ra - yim

ho- tzee- a - nu me- mitz ra - yim da - ye - nu.
v'lo ka - ra lanu et ha - yam ___ da - ye - nu.

Da- da- ye- nu ___ da- da- ye- nu ___ da- da- ye- nu da-

1.
ye- nu da- ye- nu da- ye- nu

2.
ye- nu da- ye- nu.

midwives who refused to follow Pharaoh's orders to drown newborn Israelite boys; without Yocheved, who hid her baby, Moses, for three months, then wove him a little basket so he could float safely down the river Nile; without Pharaoh's daughter, Thermutis, who defied her father, the king of all Egypt, when she rescued an Israelite child and drew Moses from the water.

And, last but not least, the Exodus never could have happened without Miriam the prophet—who watched over Moses, who brought her mother to Pharaoh's daughter, who led the singing and celebration after our safe crossing through the Sea of Reeds. Legend also tells us that Miriam found the wells that kept us alive during the forty years we wandered in the wilderness before we came into the Promised Land.

LEADER:

Let us read the following words aloud together.

EVERYONE:

Our tradition teaches that all of us must work together to end slavery, find freedom, and create a better world. In this spirit, let us each pour some water from our glasses to fill Miriam's Cup. Let us now dedicate this cup of water to the memory of Miriam, to the women of our Exodus, and to the women in our own lives who help heal us and repair our world.

You can say their names aloud if you like.

We Are All Children of God

Now you know how God saved us from slavery with signs and wonders. But before we drink another cup of wine, we remember the Egyptians who suffered such terrible plagues. As we name each plague out loud together, we can use our fingers or a spoon to take away a drop from our own cups of joy.

EVERYONE:
Blood, frogs, gnats and flies, wild beasts, cattle disease, boils, hail, locusts, darkness, and death of the firstborn.

We cannot satisfy our thirst or celebrate our freedom without remembering the sorrow of other people, who are all God's children. We are no longer slaves. But what does our freedom mean? How should we use it? To be a slave is to understand a slave; to be a stranger is to understand a stranger. Let's ask ourselves: Are there people I treat like slaves? Have I hardened my heart against a stranger? How could I change?

What Are the Most Important Symbols of the Seder?

Now that we have all lived again the story of Passover, who can tell us what these symbols of the Seder mean? You can use your own words, or read these definitions.

What is the meaning of this roasted bone [or beet]?
It reminds us that God passed over the houses of the Children of Israel when the firstborn Egyptians died.

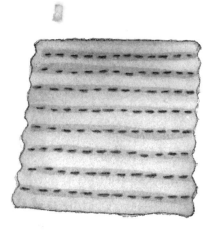

What is the meaning of this matzah?
We eat matzah to remind us that we had no time to get ready or bake bread when God rescued us from Egypt.

What is the meaning of this *maror*?
We eat *maror* to remind us how bitter it is to be a slave.

This is a good time to discuss any other questions about the Seder, the Exodus, or the customs and traditions of the Passover holiday.

SONGS OF PRAISE

We sing praises to God to give thanks for all of our blessings:

> *Could song fill our mouths as water fills the sea,*
> *And could joy flood our tongues like countless waves,*
> *Could our lips utter praise as limitless as the sky,*
> *And could our eyes match the splendor of the sun,*
> *Could we soar with arms like eagles' wings*
> *And run with gentle grace, like the swiftest deer,*
> *Never could we fully state our gratitude*
> *For one ten-thousandth of the lasting love*
> *Which is Your precious blessing, dear God,*
> *Granted to our ancestors and to us.*

Thank you, God, for everything you have done for us: for taking us from slavery to freedom, from sadness to happiness, from pain to joy, from darkness to light.

THE SECOND CUP OF WINE

Blessing for the Wine

We praise You, Eternal God, Creator of the universe, who creates the fruit of the vine.

Now we drink the second cup of wine. Be sure to lean back and rest to show you are no longer a slave, for in ancient times slaves served others, and only free people could recline while they ate.

LEADER:

We all wash our hands again to help us feel pure and to remind us how important it is to make a fresh start as a brand-new cycle of life and growth begins. This time we say the blessing.

Blessing for Washing Our Hands

We praise You, Eternal God, Creator of the universe, who makes us holy by Your commandments and commands us to wash our hands.

LEADER:

We always thank God for giving us bread to eat.

Blessing for Bread

Blessed are You, Eternal God, Creator of the universe, who brings forth bread from the earth.

בָּרוּךְ אַתָּה יְיָ אֱלֹהֵינוּ מֶלֶךְ
הָעוֹלָם הַמּוֹצִיא לֶחֶם מִן־הָאָרֶץ.

Ba-RUKH A-TAH A-do-NAI, E-lo-HAY-nu, ME-lekh ha-o-LAM, ha-mo-TSEE LE-hem min ha-AH-retz.

But now we thank God for this different and important kind of bread called matzah.

Blessing for Eating Matzah

Blessed are You, Eternal God, Creator of the universe, who makes our lives holy with Your commandments, and commands us to eat matzah.

בָּרוּךְ אַתָּה יְיָ אֱלֹהֵינוּ מֶלֶךְ
הָעוֹלָם אֲשֶׁר קִדְּשָׁנוּ בְּמִצְוֹתָיו וְצִוָּנוּ
עַל־אֲכִילַת מַצָּה.

Ba-RUKH A-TAH A-do-NAI, E-lo-HAY-nu, ME-lekh
ha-o-LAM ah-SHER kid-SHA-nu b'MITZ-vo-TAV v'tsee-VA-nu
al a-khee-LOT ma-TZAH.

Now I will break up the top matzah and give pieces to everyone. Let's also pass around the *maror* and *haroset* to share.

Almost two thousand years ago, Rabbi Hillel taught us to eat matzah and *maror* together to fulfill the commandments of the Torah—to feel as if we, each of us, taste again tonight both the bitterness of slavery and the sweetness of freedom.

You can make a "Hillel sandwich" by putting *maror* and *haroset* between two *matzot*. When we eat matzah and *maror* we taste the bread of affliction—the bread of sorrow and poverty—and the bitterness of slavery. *Haroset* adds the sweet taste of freedom and reminds us how God saved us.

Blessing for Eating *Maror*

*Blessed are You, Eternal God, Creator of the universe,
who makes our lives holy with Your commandments and
commands us to eat* maror.

בָּרוּךְ אַתָּה יְיָ אֱלֹהֵינוּ מֶלֶךְ
הָעוֹלָם אֲשֶׁר קִדְּשָׁנוּ בְּמִצְוֹתָיו
וְצִוָּנוּ עַל־אֲכִילַת מָרוֹר.

Ba-RUKH A-TAH A-do-NAI, E-lo-HAY-nu, ME-lekh
ha-o-LAM a-SHER kid-SHA-nu b'MITZ-vo-TAV v'tsee-VA-nu
al a-khee-LOT ma-ROR.

TIME TO EAT!

Tonight we can lean back while we enjoy every delicious bite
of our Passover meal. This is because we are free. And now, let's
enjoy our meal and the sweet taste of freedom.

Serve and eat the meal, including dessert.

After the Meal

Searching for the *Afikoman*

LEADER:

We usually end our evening meal with dessert. But many things are different tonight. Even though we already ate dessert, the *Afikoman* must be the very last thing we eat at our Seder meal. But where is it? Will you help us find it?

Search for the *Afikoman*.

Now that we've enjoyed the fun and excitement of finding the *Afikoman*, I will break it into tiny pieces for everyone to share. Let the taste linger in your mouth to remind you of all we saw and heard tonight.

Blessing After Our Meal

Thank you, God, for the food we enjoyed. May God bless this home, the people at this table, and all our loved ones. May God bring peace to all homes and to every nation.

Now we drink the third cup of wine together. As we recite the blessing and then drink, remember those who are not free to have a Seder. We wish they could be with us tonight to join our festival of freedom. We hope people all over the world will soon be free.

THE THIRD CUP OF WINE

Blessing for the Wine

Blessed are You, Eternal God, Creator of the universe, who creates the fruit of the vine.

ELIJAH'S CUP

This beautiful wine cup is placed in the center of our table waiting for an honored guest, waiting for Elijah the prophet.

Long ago, Elijah protected the Jews from an evil king and queen. He healed the sick and helped the weak. When his days on earth were over, legend says Elijah rode up into the sky on a chariot of fire.

Legends also tell us that this mysterious man returns to earth to help the helpless, to answer the unanswerable, and to remind us that some day, when the Messiah comes, all people will be free.

All over the world, in every Jewish home, children open the

door on Passover to invite Elijah to enter. Perhaps tonight he will honor us and enter our home. Our hope makes a bridge between heaven and earth.

LEADER:

Go. Open the door to welcome him as we read these words:

Behold, I will send you Elijah the prophet, and he will turn the hearts of the parents to the children and the hearts of the children to the parents before the coming of the great and awesome Day of the Lord

[Malachi 3:23–24]

As we close the door, we sing Elijah's song:

Elijah the prophet, Elijah the prophet,
May he come soon, in our day.

Eliyahu Hanavi

Traditional
arr. Rogerio Marx

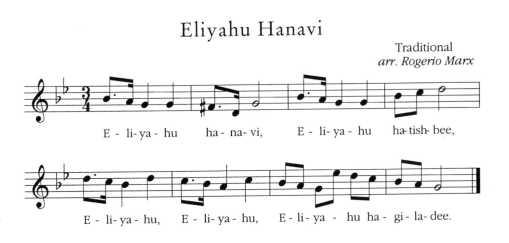

E - li- ya - hu   ha - na- vi,   E - li- ya - hu   ha- tish- bee,

E - li- ya - hu,   E - li- ya - hu,   E - li- ya - hu ha - gi - la- dee.

Look at Elijah's cup: Did any of the wine disappear? Did he come? Is he here?

It is said that in each generation Elijah the prophet returns disguised as a poor, oppressed stranger. He knows by the way people treat him whether the world is ready for the Messiah. What do you think—are we ready yet?

Concluding Our Seder

LEADER:
Together, we drink the fourth and last cup of wine, full of hope that we will all share the blessings of peace and freedom.

The Fourth Cup of Wine

Blessing for the Wine

Blessed are You, Eternal God, Creator of the universe, who creates the fruit of the vine.

Tonight we tell the story of our Exodus from Egypt to you, our children; someday you will tell it to your children; and someday they will tell it again and again to their children and their children's children.

This is our hope: that each of us will be a link in the chain that stretches from God to Moses, to Miriam, to me; that you will become strong links in the chain that stretches from generation to generation, like hands holding hands across the years.

As our Seder ends, we say *shalom*, peace, with our lips and our hearts. We pray for peace, for us, for everyone. Next year in Jerusalem: next year may everyone be free.

Some people mean they want to celebrate Passover in the actual city of Jerusalem when they say, "Next year in Jerusalem." But others are expressing the hope that they will be together again at Passover with all their loved ones.

And for many people, saying, "Next year in Jerusalem" is another way of saying they hope by next year to live in a world that offers safety and peace, freedom and plenty, to all people, all over the world.

"Khad Gadya"

This song tells a Passover story that grows and grows—kind of like a Jewish "Old MacDonald Had a Farm." There are serious interpretations of this cumulative song, written in Aramaic, involving the history of the Jewish people and the yearning for the Messiah to come. For example, the *khad gadya*, the little goat, can be said to represent the children of Israel, and the other animals some of our many enemies. But for now, just relax and enjoy!

Everyone can join the fun and it's a delightful way to end your Seder. Here's how: Assign individuals or small groups to act out each character or event in the song with gestures and even sound effects. For example, the goat bleats, the cat says meow, the stick bangs, the fire sizzles. The last few are harder so you'll need to be creative (some suggestions: water flows, the ox lows, the butcher cuts, the Angel of Death flaps arms like wings).

An only goat, an only goat my father bought for two zuzim.
Khad gadya, khad gadya.

Then came the cat
And ate the goat my father bought for two zuzim.
Khad gadya, khad gadya.

Then came the dog
And bit the cat
That ate the goat my father bought for two zuzim.
Khad gadya, khad gadya.

Then came the stick
And beat the dog
That bit the cat
That ate the goat my father bought for two zuzim.
Khad gadya, khad gadya.

Then came the fire
And burned the stick
That beat the dog
That bit the cat
That ate the goat my father bought for two zuzim.
Khad gadya, khad gadya.

Then came the water
And quenched the fire
That burned the stick
That beat the dog
that bit the cat
That ate the goat my father bought for two zuzim.
Khad gadya, khad gadya.

Then came the ox
And drank the water
That quenched the fire
That burned the stick
That beat the dog
That bit the cat
That ate the goat my father bought for two zuzim.
Khad gadya, khad gadya.

Then came the butcher
And killed the ox
That drank the water
That quenched the fire
That burned the stick
That beat the dog
The bit the cat
That ate the goat my father bought for two zuzim.
Khad gadya, khad gadya.

Then came the Angel of Death
And slew the butcher
That killed the ox
That drank the water
That quenched the fire
That burned the stick
That beat the dog

That bit the cat
That ate the goat my father bought for two zuzim.
Khad gadya, khad gadya.

Then came the Holy One, blessed be God,
And destroyed the Angel of Death
That slew the butcher
That killed the ox
That drank the water
That quenched the fire
That burned the stick
That beat the dog
That bit the cat
That ate the goat my father bought for two zuzim.
Khad gadya, khad gadya.

Khad Gadya

Traditional
arr. Rogerio Marx

Khad gad - ya ——— khad gad - ya,

khad gad - ya ——— khad gad - ya. Deez -

von a - ba bi - tray— zu- zay. Khad gad ya ———

khad gad - ya. V' - a - ta shoon- ra v' -

akh - la l' - gad- ya deez- von a - ba bi - tray— zu- zay.

Khad gad - ya ——— khad gad - ya.

How Children
Can Participate in Your Seder

Children love to participate. Helping you, more than anything else, makes them feel important and connected. So try to find age-appropriate ways to involve each child in the preparations and celebration of your Seder. You, of course, are the best judge of which children will enjoy these suggested activities.

ACTIVITIES BEFORE THE SEDER

• Help with cleaning and vacuuming.

• Help clean their own rooms. (Don't forget the crumbs!)

• Help bring *hametz* to a soup kitchen so hungry people can enjoy eating it.

• Help search for *hametz* (see pages 5–7). An adult must supervise the use of a candle.

• Mix salt and water for dipping (see page 10).

• Help make *haroset* (see page 10).

• Help prepare the Seder plate (see pages 9–10).

• Put three *matzot* on a plate and make a cover. (One way is to have the children color with crayons on a plain white cloth, then have a grown-up use wax paper and a hot iron to set the colors. You can probably think of your own decorations.)

• Polish Elijah's cup, or decorate one themselves.

• Help choose and polish Miriam's Cup (or decorate one).

• Place candles and holders on the Seder table.

• Help set the Seder table (see pages 11–12).

• Make place cards with guests' names.

• Create a welcome sign for the front door.

ADDITIONAL ACTIVITIES DURING THE SEDER

• Hide the *Afikoman* (or help find it).

• Help pass plates of greens, matzah, *maror*, etc. during the Seder.

• Bring pitcher, bowl, and towel for washing hands to each guest.

• In the Sephardic tradition, children often act out the drama of the Exodus as the story is read during the Seder (see pages 29–41). This is a wonderful way to bring the ancient story right into the present and make it actually "happen" to you. Be sure to plan ahead with your children if you'd like to add this feature.

Gather towels, headgear, robes, walking staffs, sandals, and other costume materials.

Assign the major roles (Moses, Miriam, Pharaoh, Yocheved, Pharaoh's daughter) and stress the importance of other roles.

Decide together where Egypt, the wilderness, the sea, and other important "sets" will be.

• Traditionally, the youngest child asks the Four Questions. In some cases, however, this puts too much pressure on children, so handle this moment with sensitivity. (The best way is, of course, to discuss it beforehand.) Consider some of the many variations: all children or all guests can recite or sing the questions together; individuals can volunteer to ask the questions; a child of Bar or Bat Mitzvah age could be chosen; or . . . create your own custom.

• Children—and even some of the adults—at your Seder may enjoy acting out the ten plagues at the proper moments as you tell the Passover story (see pages 33–37). They can hop like frogs, buzz like flies, munch like locusts, fall dead like the Egyptian firstborn. This dramatic play can help bring the Seder story alive.

• One child (or all the children) can open the door for Elijah.

• Invite children and grown-ups to join the fun of singing and dramatizing *"Khad Gadya."*